Why would anyone go to Trona?

Bryce Steven Banks

Copyright © 2015 Bryce Steven Banks
All rights reserved.
ISBN-13: 978-1943417049

DEDICATION

This book is dedicated to my grandparents Hershel and Zelia Stevens, and their Trona-raised children, Patty, Joel, David, and Douglas.

The lowest, driest, and hottest place in North America is Death Valley. Not far from Death Valley is the town of Trona. Trona is also very hot and dry and, because of the Chemical plant, is one of the smelliest towns in North America. It seems fair to ask: why would anyone go to Trona?

In 1933 my Grandpa Hershel went to Trona from Indiana to work in the plant because it was the only place he could get a job. In 1935 my Grandma Zelia went to Trona from Georgia to be with Grandpa Hershel.

AERIAL PHOTOGRAPHS DURING THE STRIKE
The First Three Weeks — Feb. 1 through Feb. 21, 1972

KAISER STEEL

Hershel and Zelia's first child was Patty. In 1953 Patty left Trona to attend BYU where she met and married Ray Banks. They raised their family in Fontana, a factory town a few hours south of Trona. The factory in Fontana was Kaiser Steel. Although Kaiser didn't make the town stink, it did make it very smoggy. On the worst days schools would cancel recess because the air was unsafe to breathe. A question for another time: "Why would anyone go to Fontana?"

Why would anyone go to Trona? For the Banks kids it was a favorite vacation or holiday trip. The kids loved going to Trona to visit their Grandpa and Grandma Stevens. On the ride the kids would watch for signs that they were getting closer.

The first sign was the whoop-de-dos. This is where the road quickly goes up and then right back down again. It is like being on a miles long roller coaster ride. The kids always squealed with delight.

The next sign they would watch for was the Fish rocks. Where else can you find fish in the desert? Only on the road to Trona.

They knew they were getting really close when they saw the Pinnacles. They look like something from another planet.

Finally, even if it was after dark, they knew they had made it to Trona by the smell. That awful smell meant one of two things. Either someone had cut the cheese (again) or they had arrived in Trona. They knew for sure when they rolled down the windows to air out the car and the smell outside the car was worse than the smell inside the car.

Sure, you could fly to Trona (there is an airport), but when going to Trona getting there is half the fun.

Since Uncle Joel and Aunt Pauline also lived in Trona the kids spent a lot of time playing with their cousins.

Being a desert, most plants won't grow in Trona. There are no lawns- just some ugly old tamarisk trees. The trees provide a bit of shade, and were the source of the switches that Grandma Zelia would use when the grandkids were in need of a whipping. Fortunately, Uncle Joel's kids, Leroy, Ronnie, and Stevie Stevens, were most often the recipients of such discipline. They seemed to always be in need of a good whipping.

Sometimes the kids would walk out to the golf course behind the plant and hunt for lost balls and tees.

Sometimes they would hike up to the T on the mountain.

On really hot days they would go to Valley Wells to cool off in the salt water pool.

The Company Club house was right across the street from Grandma's house and the kids would sometimes sneak in through the basement windows to play in the bowling alley.

Once in a while they would make a trip to the dump. Although you were only supposed to drop things off the kids would usually bring home some "treasure" that they had found in the sometimes smoldering trash heap.

My grandfather earned a good living working in Trona. The time my siblings and I spent in Trona has given us many fond and lasting memories. It holds a special place in our hearts.

Why would anyone go to Trona?

There is truly nowhere else like it. In fact if this sign (which was once posted on the road outside Trona) is correct, Trona is out of this world. A sentiment I can agree with. Perhaps the real question ought to be: Why doesn't everyone want to go to Trona?

Trona Trivia

Tornadoes are a rarity in California, but not unheard of. Seen more often in the desert around Trona are dust devils. The high school is the home of the Trona Tornadoes.

The Blue and White Tornadoes

The Blue and White Tornado gang is on the move today.
The tenderfoot will surely learn to stay out of its way.
The boys and girls of Trona High will cheer their fav' rite play, and when the team comes on the field they'll all stand up and say, Here come the Blue and White Tornadoes. Here come the sons of Trona High. With colors flying, with hearts undying. they will surely do or die. Come on and fight, fight, fight for Trona, The Blue and White are up to stay, Come on Tornadoes! Come on Tornadoes! We know you'll clean the field today.

Arr. by W. E. Olberg, Words & Music by L.A. Blackmun, Published in 1948

The Trona Tornadoes play on the only dirt football field in the country. Locals know it as "The pit".

At one time Trona had its own currency.

The American Potash & Chemical Corporation conceived, planned, built, and owned the town. From 1931-1957 the company issued "Trona Dollars" and Trona tokens.

Shortly after WWII Trona employers posted Help Wanted Ads around California offering "EXTRA GOOD WAGES".

17 Help Wanted Male

T-R-O-N-A
Work Comfortably in a Small Plant Without Transportation Worries

Trona is a modern community having theatre, swimming & picnic resort, employes' club, bowling, tennis, golf, stores, churches, dormitories, coffee shop, mess hall.

THERE IS A JOB OPEN IN TRONA WHICH WILL JUST SUIT YOU.

5 Men, no exp. needed, to train for plant operation jobs. Fine opportunity for good afterwar jobs at EXTRA GOOD WAGES.
8 Men to help in shipping dept.
6 Men to help in mechanical dept.
4 Men for chemistry lab. dept. (1 yr. college required.)
Comb. Welder—Machinist.
Steam Crane Engineer.

ROOM - BOARD - FARE ADVANCED

AMERICAN POTASH & CHEMICAL CORP.
SEE TRONA MAN
San Bernardino U.S.E.S., 355 D St.

Mill Helpers ......88c Hr.
Quarrymen ....93c Hr.
No experience required.
BOARD, ROOM AND TRANSPORTATION ADVANCED
Permanent Desert Industry
For Information
WEST END CHEMICAL CO.
355 D St.

On at least two occasions mail was sent to Trona by rocket.

The Rocket Research Institute fired 11-foot rockets across Searles Lake to Trona as a preliminary test of long-distance mail delivery at high speeds.

From certain vantage points the salt on the surface of the lake can look just like snow. In fact, it rarely snows in Trona. Old timers recall fondly however the storm of January 1949 when there was more than six inches of snowfall. With the classrooms ill-equipped to handle the cold, students were directed to gather in the auditorium. For the week that the snow stayed on the ground, students passed the time dancing and participating in other group activities.

Searles Valley Minerals utilizes a unique mining technique to extract the minerals from beneath the surface of Searles Lake. After extracting the chemicals in its plants it returns the partially depleted brine to the lake where it continues to do what it does naturally-dissolving additional minerals for future production.

Before the railroad was built 20 mule teams hauled large wagons of borax from Searles Lake to the harbor at San Pedro. You can still purchase 20 mule team Borax at stores everywhere.

The wild burros you might see roaming in the Trona area should not be confused with the mules used to haul borax. They are different animals altogether. The burros are descendants of pack animals used by early prospectors.

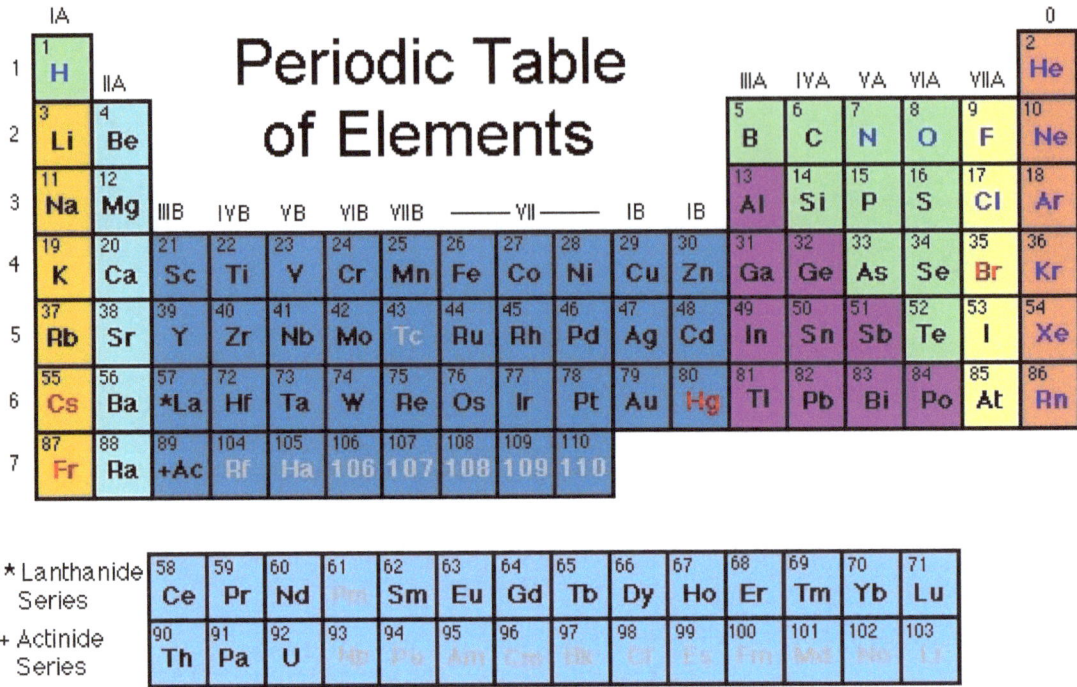

Searles Lake contains 98 of the 104 naturally occurring chemical elements.

Each year on the second weekend of October the Searles Lake Gem & Mineral Society sponsors the Gem-o-Rama in Trona. Rock and gem collectors from around the world come to Trona for the one time each year that the lake is open to the public to collect crystals.

$$Na_3(HCO_3)(CO_3) - 2H_2O > Au$$

Translation: Trona is greater than Gold.

Trona   >   Gold

The value of the minerals taken from the Searles Lake exceeds the value of all the gold found during the **California Gold Rush** (1848–1855).

Though Searles Lake has been mined over the last century and a half, Trona only became an official town when the Trona Post Office opened on March 27, 1914.

In 2014 a three day celebration was held to celebrate the town's 100th birthday. Displays, a parade, a car show and other festivities were enjoyed by current and former Tronans from near and far. From all accounts it was reported to be Tronariffic!

www.ingramcontent.com/pod-product-compliance
Lightning Source LLC
Chambersburg PA
CBHW041227040426
42444CB00002B/73